Reptile World

Pythons

by Cari Meister

Bullfrog Books

Ideas for Parents and Teachers

Bullfrog Books let children practice reading informational text at the earliest reading levels. Repetition, familiar words, and photo labels support early readers.

Before Reading

- Discuss the cover photo. What does it tell them?
- Look at the picture glossary together. Read and discuss the words.

Read the Book

- "Walk" through the book and look at the photos. Let the child ask questions. Point out the photo labels.
- Read the book to the child, or have him or her read independently.

After Reading

- Prompt the child to think more. Ask: Have you ever seen a python? Had it eaten recently? How could you tell?

Bullfrog Books are published by Jump!
5357 Penn Avenue South
Minneapolis, MN 55419
www.jumplibrary.com

Library of Congress Cataloging-in-Publication Data

Meister, Cari, author.
Pythons / by Cari Meister.
Pages cm. — (Bullfrog books. Reptile world)
Summary: "This photo-illustrated book for beginning readers describes the physical features and behaviors of pythons. Includes picture glossary and index."—Provided by publisher.
Audience: Ages 5–8.
Audience: K to grade 3.
Includes index.
ISBN 978-1-62031-198-1 (hardcover: alk. paper) —
ISBN 978-1-62496-285-1 (ebook)
1. Pythons—Juvenile literature. I. Title.
QL666.O67M45 2015
597.96'78—dc23

2014042732

Series Editor: Jenny Fretland VanVoorst
Series Designer: Ellen Huber
Book Designer: Michelle Sonnek
Photo Researcher: Michelle Sonnek

Photo Credits: All photos by Shutterstock except: 123RF, 4, 23bl; age fotostock, 8–9; Alamy, 15, 23br; Corbis, 10; Getty, 18–19; Nature Picture Library, 6–7, 20–21; Science Source Images, 14; Thinkstock, 1, 12–13, 22.

Printed in the United States of America at Corporate Graphics in North Mankato, Minnesota.

Table of Contents

A Good Hunter 4
Parts of a Python 22
Picture Glossary 23
Index 24
To Learn More 24

A Good Hunter

A python lies
in the sun.

He is cold-blooded.
He needs the sun.
It gives him energy.

Now he is ready.

He can hunt.

He goes to the river.

He is a good swimmer.
He looks for food.

He eats birds.

He eats lizards.

He eats mammals.

A deer drinks.

The snake swims.

He is quiet.

He grabs.
He has strong jaws.
They hold the deer.

He wraps.

He squeezes.

The deer
cannot breathe.

It dies.

The snake opens his jaws.

He swallows.

It is a big meal.

He will not eat
for many days.

Parts of a Python

scales
Pythons have small, smooth scales.

eyes
Pythons have poor eyesight.

tongue
Pythons have a forked tongue that helps them sense things in the air.

heat pits
Pythons have holes near their nostrils that help them sense heat from other animals.

Picture Glossary

cold-blooded
An animal that has the same body temperature as the air around it.

mammal
A kind of animal that has fur or hair and feeds milk to its young.

lizard
A kind of reptile that walks on four legs and has dry, scaly skin.

wrap
To go around something.

Index

birds 10
cold-blooded 5
deer 12, 14, 16
food 8
hunting 6
jaws 14, 19
lizards 11
mammals 11
river 6
squeezing 16
sun 4, 5
swimming 8, 12

To Learn More

Learning more is as easy as 1, 2, 3.

1) Go to www.factsurfer.com
2) Enter "pythons" into the search box.
3) Click the "Surf" button to see a list of websites.

With factsurfer.com, finding more information is just a click away.